Five Women

FIVE WOMEN
Lessons in Forgiveness and Usefulness
Denise Rinker Adler

Tyndale House
Publishers, Inc.
Wheaton, Illinois

Scripture verses quoted in this book
are taken from *The Living Bible*
(© 1971 by Tyndale House Publishers, Wheaton, Ill.)
unless otherwise indicated.
Verses marked KJV are from the
King James Version.

Library of Congress Catalog Card Number 79-92973
ISBN 0-8423-0874-1
Copyright © 1980 by Denise Adler.
All rights reserved.
First printing, April 1980.
Printed in the United States of America.

CONTENTS

How to Use This Discussion Guide   7

Introduction   *9*

Lesson 1   **Tamar**   *13*

Lesson 2   **Rahab**   *19*

Lesson 3   **Ruth**   *27*

Lesson 4   **Bathsheba**   *37*

Lesson 5   **Mary, the Mother of Jesus**   *43*

Lesson 6   **Review**   *55*

Lesson 7   **The Ideal Woman**/*Proverbs 31:10-31*   *61*

How to Use This Discussion Guide

If you are a leader for this study, we would encourage you to examine the material in these introductory sections carefully.

Personal Preparation

(1) Prepare thoroughly. Outline the material you will be presenting. Read and study *each* day during the week prior to the class.

(2) Take full advantage of all reference works, commentaries, and good resource materials. Take plenty of notes.

(3) Pray much! Search your own heart for anything that could stand in the way of God's blessing your service for him. Trust him fully to use you. "You didn't choose me! I chose you! I appointed you to go and reproduce lovely fruit always" (John 15:16). Ask God to make his love flow through you to each member of the class.

(4) Write discussion questions designed to provoke thought and stimulate serious digging into the Word. Some questions may have answers taken from chapter and verse in the passage; others

may come from other sources or Bible portions. Most questions will center around: what does it say? what does it say to me? how does it apply to my life?

(5) Remember that Christian commitment means taking the responsibilities that God has given you seriously enough to carry them out completely. This commitment is the key to leadership.

Characteristics and Procedures of Bible Discussion Leaders

(1) Help the group apply the lesson to everyday needs. Don't just talk theory; present life!

(2) Be a good listener. Make it a point to give a careful hearing to what each participant is saying.

(3) Accept all constructive criticism. Use it to become an even better leader.

(4) Always be courteous. Avoid embarrassing any member of the group.

(5) Share personal experiences that relate to the lesson. But avoid talking too much.

(6) Do not be afraid to be enthusiastic about the subject.

(7) Let the class know that you are available for further (and private) talk and prayer.

(8) Maintain an atmosphere of friendliness and helpfulness.

(9) Come to class well-prepared and well-prayed.

(10) Keep the group's attention. Do not allow sideline conversations. Also, help the group stay on the subject.

(11) Encourage shy, quiet members to take part, but do not demand or force their participation.

(12) Clarify wrong answers *tactfully*. Never say, "Your answer is wrong."

(13) Never answer your own question.

(14) Never criticize any specific church or denomination.

(15) Remember the primary objective for the class: to direct class members toward Jesus Christ.

Introduction

Tamar shocks us by the way she went about propagating Judah's line. Yet we have to acknowledge that a fruitful race followed. God kept his promise, and the lifeline in the lineage of Jesus stayed pure and clean. God knew exactly what he was doing. Haven't you found that he never makes a mistake? You can trust him to work out your problems, big and small. As you study these five women, your faith in him should be strengthened to believe as a small child believes. "You said it, Lord Jesus, and I believe it." It's that simple.

It is true that God's choosing you to become a member of his family was by grace alone; otherwise Judah would never have been chosen. The fact that Judah was a Jew and Tamar a Gentile shows that both Jews and Gentiles were to share in the blessing of the Good News.

Rahab is referred to as being the wife of Salmon, one of the two spies she sheltered. In turn, she became the mother of Boaz who married Ruth. Their son was Obed, the grandfather of King David. Salmon was the pride of the house of Judah. Thus Rahab, the heathen harlot, married into one of the leading families of Israel and became an ancestress of our Lord, other foreign ancestresses being Tamar, Ruth, and Bathsheba.

It has been suggested that the word "harlot" can be translated "innkeeper." This would make Rahab the landlady of a wayside tavern. But she was still known as a harlot who gave herself to every man who wanted her.

She took her life in her hands when she befriended the spies so they could reach Joshua with their report on the Promised Land. The red "token" she placed at her window was a signal to the outside world that she believed in the triumph of Jehovah. It resembled the promise in Exodus 12:13—"When I see the blood I will pass over you." As the scarlet line, because of its color and sign of safety, spoke of the sacrificial work of Christ (Hebrews 9:19, 22), so the ground of our assurance of personal salvation is not based on feelings within, but the "token" without.

"By faith—because she believed God and his power—Rahab the harlot did not die with all the others in her city when they refused to obey God, for she gave a friendly welcome to the spies" (Hebrews 11:31).

Ruth rose from obscurity to riches. The first glimpse we have of her is as a young widow robbed by death of her husband. It took God's grace to help Ruth befriend a bitter Naomi as she left to go back to her own land. Ruth's loyalty helped change Naomi's sourness into sweetness. We all have friends like Ruth who demonstrate to us the love of God, and others like Orpah whose fair-weather friendship quickly leaves us. The beauty of Ruth's character is shown in her words, "Don't make me leave you," though Naomi had twice asked her to do exactly that. It was not chance that brought Boaz and Ruth together. God directs the steps of his children. From Ruth's outstanding qualities of unselfishness and loyalty we learn how true happiness can be built into our lives.

Bathsheba belonged to a religious family. She was the daughter of Eliam, the son of Ahithophel. Eliam was one of David's loyal officers. Bathsheba became the wife of Uriah, also one of David's most loyal men. After the murder of Uriah, she became the wife of David and the mother of Solomon. Included in the genealogy of Jesus, she was identified as "the widow of Uriah" (Matthew 1:6).

Her sin was forgiven and she was given divine favor. She was virtuous and wise as well as beautiful. After the birth of her son Solomon, who found favor with God and man, little was said about her. A lesson we can learn from her life is that she did not let sin ruin her entire life. She used her mistakes as guides to help her become a better person.

Mary was chosen by God the Father to be the mother of his Son, Jesus Christ. No woman on the face of the earth has had as much honor as Mary. She was an outstanding woman. The more you study her life, the greater her example becomes to you. She is not divine—she does not stand apart from the rest of the human race—she was not sinless. She recognized her need of deliverance from sin and guilt when she sang, "My spirit hath rejoiced in God my Saviour" (Luke 1:47, KJV). Let the Holy Spirit, your teacher, implant in your life the example of Mary's life, her love for her children, and most of all her love for her Lord.

LESSON 1
Tamar

NOTES

(Read Genesis 38:6-30; Ruth 4:12, 1 Chronicles 2:4; Matthew 1:3. Note especially Genesis 38:26—"She hath been more righteous than I.")

Tamar's scheme to produce an heir surprises us, though it resembles current events. We wonder why God used Tamar, a pagan woman, to be in the bloodline of Jesus Christ. But God knew Tamar's faith and honored her desire to be in his family. God never makes a mistake; his timing is always perfect. Have you found this out in your life?

The custom of that day gave Tamar every right to have an heir, but Judah held out on her. He didn't keep his promise to give her in marriage to his youngest son, Shelah. The law didn't change because of this, nor did Tamar's rights change. This story is a historical record of the lives of primitive people living in a primitive time.

Tamar tricked Judah, but then again Judah asked for it by his actions. It almost seemed like it was his own idea. Only God's grace could bring anything good out of such a situation.

This story of Tamar reminds us that in God's eyes there are no ordinary people. We are all special. Every one of us can be used by

God. No one should feel "not good enough" or "inadequate" or "lacking in education." Our salvation is a gift of God—"by grace ye are saved" (Ephesians 2:5).

Tamar was just an ordinary woman, not especially noble, but lovely to look at, and a very determined person. She acted as a woman. She had a sincere desire to belong to God's people, but she used the wrong method: trickery. Judah was motivated by sensual lust. He was not honest until he was humiliated by Tamar. His honesty came out only under duress. "Pride goes before destruction and haughtiness before a fall" (Proverbs 16:18).

Application: Today I will be absolutely honest in all my dealings with my fellowmen.

_____

Your signature

QUESTIONS

(1) What does 1 Chronicles 2:4 tell you about Tamar?

_____

_____

_____

(2) Why was Tamar's action "more righteous" than that of Judah's (Genesis 38:26)?

_____

_____

_____

(3) a. What motivated Tamar's plan of action?

_____

_____

_____

b.   How did she plan to justify her actions?

_____

_____

_____

(4) a.   Was the genealogy of Jesus Christ (Matthew 1:1-17) made up only of the choice or holiest of people and races? Why or why not?

_____

_____

   b.   How many women were included in the genealogy of Jesus and who were they?

_____

_____

(5) These people lived under an "eye for an eye" kind of justice. How does that enter into the story of Tamar?

_____

_____

_____

(6) What did God do directly at the time of their misbehavior? What did he do later?

_____

_____

_____

(7) Bishop Hall says, "God's election is only by grace, for otherwise Judah would never have been chosen." Judah was a Hebrew, but Tamar was considered a Gentile. Thus her parentage of Perez (Matthew 1:3) can be looked upon as a foreshadowing of the fact that both Jews and Gentiles were to share in the blessings of

the gospel. So what did Tamar have to do with the work and mission of Jesus Christ?

_____

_____

_____

_____

(8) What can we learn from this story? How can we apply it to our lives today?

_____

_____

_____

_____

(9) Why do you think Tamar was included in God's "Who's Who"?

_____

_____

_____

(10) Did she get into God's family by works? Explain.

_____

_____

_____

_____

(11) Describe Tamar in your own words.

_____

_____

_____

Dear Lord, I uplift to thee
my confusion and defects,
my faded hope and my bitterness of heart.
In thy hands I place them.
In thy love I release them.
Christ, receive them!
God, forgive them!
Spirit, restore them!
Gather up the broken fragments of my life,
so that in thee my life may become
complete and whole and glad.
Amen!

LESSON 2
Rahab

NOTES

Rahab was a harlot who turned into a believer. Read Joshua 2—6; Hebrews 11:31; and James 2:25.

The author of Hebrews named Rahab as one of that great "cloud of witnesses" (12:1, KJV) who lived lives of faith. She is the only woman besides Sarah whom he names as an example of faith. James mentions her as one who is worthy because of her good works (James 2:25).

God knew Rahab was a harlot, but he also saw she was a woman of faith. Until we have God in our heart, it is filled with darkness. "All have sinned, and come short of the glory of God" (Romans 3:23, KJV). But "God did not send his Son into the world to condemn it, but to save it" (John 3:17).

As God saved Rahab and her entire family, so will he save you and me and our entire families if we believe in him. Notice that God did not wait until Rahab became a perfect woman to start his redemptive work in her heart. He knew her need and he saw her faith. We don't understand Rahab and why she did the things she did. We don't know why she was a prostitute, but God understood and stepped in and changed her life. He knew her heart was loving toward him, as he knows how your heart is toward him. He created her and loved her and she accepted his love and protection. She did not fail him, and she did not fail his spies—she hid them.

On the seventh day the victory was won—the Israelites had seen the red rope over her door. Caleb and Salmon found her inside her house, her family around her, waiting to be rescued. The promise had been kept, and Rahab and her family went back with the conquerors to Gilgal.

Rahab married Salmon, one of the spies who visited her home. She became an Israelite. She was the mother of Boaz, who married Ruth, and their grandson was King David, through the line of the Messiah, Jesus Christ.

Rahab is an example of faith with works. She was in the lineage of Jesus Christ, Son of God, proving God is no respecter of persons.

Application: God knows what I am, but he still loves me. Today I choose to accept his love and to rejoice in it.

Your signature

QUESTIONS

(1) Review last week's lesson. Share something practical that you used this past week from Tamar's life.

___

___

___

___

(2) a. What does Hebrews 11:31 say about Rahab? According to that verse, why was Rahab saved and why didn't she perish with her people?

___

b. What is God teaching us about Jesus Christ through Rahab and her escape? (Compare Joshua 2:18.)

(3) a. How did Rahab prove her faith in her Redeemer?

b. Have you ever risked something for your faith? Tell about it.

(4) a. Who does secular history identify as the two spies Rahab hid in the flax drying on the roof of her house?

b. What did she tell these men (Joshua 2:9-11)?

___

(5) a. Who did Rahab want saved beside herself? Why?

___

b. How do you account for the fact that Rahab, of all her people, found a way to be saved? Give Scripture if you can.

___

(6) a. According to James 2:24-26, was she justified before God by her actions? Why or why not?

___

b. In Joshua 2:14 what offer was given to her?

___

(7) a. What important information did she give the two men to ensure their safety in getting away? Was her advice accepted by the two men? Why or why not?

_____

_____

_____

_____

_____

b. Can you find a lesson in the story of Rahab for the spiritual safety of your family? Explain.

_____

_____

_____

_____

(8) Don't you suppose that the seventh day was a long and exciting one for Rahab and her family? They were watching the marching and hearing the trumpets, seeing Jericho fall into the hands of the Israelites. Share your own emotions as you read about it.

_____

_____

_____

_____

(9) a. As soon as the city was surrendered, what happened to Rahab and her family?

_____

_____

_____

_____

b. Where did she reside the rest of her life? Why?

_____

_____

_____

(10) Read Hebrews 9:19-22, which speaks of the sacrificial work of Christ. What is the basis for our assurance of salvation?

_____

_____

_____

(11) a. The red cord typified the way you can be saved and brought into right relationship with Jesus Christ. Do you need the precious blood of Jesus applied to your life? Will you ask him into your heart, right now, as you are working on this lesson?

_____

_____

b. Read Matthew 21:31, 32 and Revelation 3:20. In your own words write down what these verses say to you.

_____

_____

_____

_____

(12) Rahab was deceitful when confronted by the king of Jericho. How can you justify this in the light of Romans 3:7, 8—"God could not judge and condemn me as a sinner if my dishonesty brought him glory by pointing up his honesty in contrast to my lies. If you follow through with that idea you come to this: the worse we are, the better God likes it! But the damnation of those who say this is just."

_____

(13) What is Rahab remembered for today?

(14) What is she teaching us? List five or six things Rahab has made meaningful to you.

(15) a. From Matthew 1, where is Rahab listed in the genealogy of Jesus Christ?

b. What other women are listed? How many are Jews? How many are Gentiles?

(16) Why do you think Rahab is listed in God's "Who's Who"?

(17) What have you learned about the life of Jesus Christ from Rahab's life?

_____

_____

_____

(18) a. Does your heart cry for the salvation of your family as Rahab's did for hers? Why or why not?

_____

_____

_____

b. How important is the salvation that Jesus gives to you and yours? How often do you and I ask and believe for their salvation?

_____

_____

c. Do you daily ask God to make you a channel through which the Holy Spirit can work? Are you conscious of the fact that he is working in you and through you, or do you just hope so?

_____

_____

d. What will it profit you and me if we gain the whole world but our family is not in Heaven with us?

_____

LESSON 3
Ruth

NOTES

We usually think of Ruth as a very young woman, but we must remember that she had been married for ten years before her husband died and had been a widow for a considerable time before she arrived in Bethlehem. The people of the East regarded her as a middle-aged woman. She was almost always seen with her mother-in-law, Naomi, and that is probably why we think of Ruth as young.

Ruth had the same heathen background as Orpah. She was a Moabitess and worshiped the idol Moloch until she came in contact with Naomi and her family. Ruth does not seem to stand out in Naomi's affections any more than Orpah. Naomi spoke to both in the same tone of voice (Chapter 1).

God used Ruth's affection for Naomi as a means of grace, for Naomi was the link with which God bound Ruth to his people and to his Son, Jesus, the Messiah. Her faith in God was wrapped up in her love for Naomi. She wanted to identify herself with Naomi for life and death. She respected Naomi's position as her mother-in-law and wanted to be a daughter to her. God's love is never limited and knows no bounds; but our love does, especially if we have a closed heart.

God was guiding Ruth when she walked into Boaz's field to glean wheat. God guided Naomi, and Ruth listened to her and took her advice about Boaz. Even though Ruth was a Moabitess, the people working around her eventually sensed her love and care. They probably told Boaz something like, "May the Lord make the woman who will come into your house like Rachel and Leah, who jointly built up the house of Israel."

Ruth and Boaz were married and when their child, Obed, was born Naomi praised God. At long last she had a grandchild.

Ruth received love because she gave love. Even if our love is not returned after we have given it, in God's eyes it is still love and will bear fruit. Ruth never defended herself against the people of Bethlehem. She accepted and loved them, and they learned to accept and love her. How do you act in the face of prejudice? Do you leave and go to another place? Is the grass always greener on the other side of the street in your life?

Ruth didn't know what God had planned for her. Ruth gave birth to Obed. To Obed, Jesse was born. Jesse was the father of David. Ruth was the grandmother of David, and thus an ancestress of Jesus Christ. Do you know what God has planned and prepared for you? I am sure it is something very lovely and beautiful, if you will trust him with your life completely.

Trust and obey,
for there is no other way
to be happy in Jesus
but to trust and obey.

Application: I shall not vindicate myself in any way. I will let Jesus do this for me.

Your signature

QUESTIONS

Aim: To choose to lay up treasures in Heaven, so I will have my arms full of golden sheaves to lay at the feet of the King; to choose to leave Moab behind and trust in the Lord Jesus Christ right where I am; to choose to open my heart and give and receive love.

INSTRUCTIONS: The book of Ruth is a delightful, easy book that takes about fifteen minutes to read. Read it through at least three or four times. Ask the Holy Spirit to instruct you and teach you out of its rich contents. You will love your time spent in this book and with your Lord.

(1) *Review:* Share something from last week's lesson that has become yours because you are using it in your life.

_____

_____

_____

_____

_____

(2) Notice the location of the book of Ruth in the Old Testament. What books are on either side of it? Why is this significant?

_____

_____

_____

(3) a. Read the first five verses of Ruth and list the things it tells about Naomi's family.

_____

_____

_____

    b. What impressed you most about this?

_____

_____

_____

(4) a. After ten years, why did Naomi want to return to Judah (Ruth 1:6)?

_____

b. What did she tell her daughters-in-law? Why do you think she said that at this particular time?

(5) a. How did Orpah and Ruth feel about leaving Naomi?

b. Frankly, how would your daughter-in-law react in this situation to you? Why?

c. Do you feel Orpah was wrong in turning back to her own people? Why or why not?

(6) a. Do you admire Naomi for her speech in 1:12, 13? Why or why not?

b. What was the immediate result (1:14)?

_____
_____
_____

(7) Ruth 1:16 is a classic verse. Write it in your own words. Memorize it this week.

_____
_____
_____
_____
_____

(8) a. Do you feel Naomi came back with empty hands (1:21)? Why or why not?

_____
_____
_____

b. What was her trouble?

_____
_____

c. What did she need to do with her problem?

_____
_____

(9) a. How did God honor Naomi?

_____
_____
_____

b. How did God honor Ruth?

___

(10) When did Ruth become a woman of faith? How do you know?

___

(11) a. How do you remember Orpah?

___

b. Was salvation ever extended to her in Moab? When and how?

___

c. What other Old Testament woman does she remind you of and why? (See Genesis 19:16, 26.)

___

(12) a. Why did Ruth cling to Naomi?

b. What was Ruth's background?

(13) In marrying Boaz, what happened to Ruth in regard to the lineage of Jesus Christ?

(14) Who were the five women in the royal ancestry? Write one characteristic of each that you remember them by. (See Matthew 1:1-17.)

(15) a. What qualities in Ruth's life show me what Jesus Christ is like?

b. There is a great love relationship between mother-in-law and daughter-in-law here. Can you name several other love relationships in the Bible between people?

(16) How was Naomi a witness to her two daughters-in-law?

___

___

___

___

(17) The German poet Goethe wrote that the book of Ruth is "the loveliest little idyll that tradition has transmitted to us." The entire story is a total victory for love. Why and how is this true?

___

___

___

___

(18) a. What action did Boaz and Ruth take against the prejudice of the people of Bethlehem?

___

___

___

___

b. Do you feel adequate in the face of prejudice? How do you handle racial prejudice, doctrinal prejudice, etc.?

___

___

___

___

(19) a. Name several of Ruth's characteristics which you admire. Put a check beside the ones you could use in your own life.

___

___

b. Read 2:12; Psalm 17:8; 36:7. Do you believe in divine providence? Why or why not?

LESSON 4
Bathsheba

NOTES

David had an eye for beautiful women, and Bathsheba was a beautiful woman. We do not know whether she knew she could be seen from the roof of the adjoining building or not. Regardless, she took her bath where she could be seen by anyone from a neighboring housetop and David was on the other roof watching. So Bathsheba may have been an accomplice to David's sin from the start.

When her husband, Uriah, returned to Jerusalem, she made no attempt to see him, nor did he see her. She did not charge the king with rape, and she did not confess her sin or repent. She just remained in her house and did nothing about anything pertaining to this deed. She did observe a period of mourning for Uriah after his death, but then went to live in the palace as David's wife. She didn't feel responsible to God as to how she used her beauty, a gift he had given her.

How wonderful it was that David had such a sensitive conscience that he asked forgiveness from God. In that primitive time, so long before Christ came, this was usually done by a priestly sacrifice. David went directly to God his Father and said, "Against thee, thee only, have I sinned" (Psalm 51:4, KJV). Then the prophet, Nathan, assured the king of forgiveness, saying, "The Lord has forgiven you" (2 Samuel 12:13). This gave David confidence that God had heard him, but he also had to reap what he had sown. This was a bitter, sorrowful experience in his life.

When David repented, God forgave him and called him "a man after my own heart." God gives us love, peace, and comfort when we come to him for forgiveness. He cleanses and heals us and draws us close to himself. Why are we so hesitant to ask forgiveness? God loves us dearly and hears us as we repent. David found out that guilt is necessary, for it leads to repentance and pardon. We have all sinned and come short of the glory of God; we are sinners saved by his grace.

Later Bathsheba, like David, gave the sin they had committed totally to God and permitted him to redeem it. God is always redeeming things that happen in your life and mine, if we will let him. If we will believe this and accept it, we will be able to see redemption working in our lives.

After God forgives us, it is up to us to begin to live the new life he has given us. Bathsheba became a good mother, a faithful wife and helpmate to David. Nathan the prophet stood by her often. He admired and respected her. He was an excellent judge of personality for the Lord.

Bathsheba's name appears in the genealogy of Jesus Christ, another testimony to the loving grace of God.

QUESTIONS

INSTRUCTIONS: Read 2 Samuel 11, 12; 1 Kings 1, 2; 1 Chronicles 3:1-9; and Psalm 51 several times each.

(1) *Review:* Share what you learned about Ruth from last week's lesson. What applications have you made in your life?

_____

_____

_____

(2) a. How is Bathsheba listed in the genealogy of Jesus Christ (Matthew 1)?

b. Who is she listed as married to? Why?

c. What does 2 Samuel 11:3 tell us about Bathsheba?

d. What is the overall picture the Bible gives of Bathsheba?

(3) How is God's mercy revealed in her story?

(4) a. What first precaution did Bathsheba neglect (especially as a woman)?

b. Can you apply this precaution to your own life? Why and how?

_____

_____

_____

c. What does the Bible tell us about Bathsheba's beauty?

_____

_____

_____

(5) Can we lay all the guilt for this sin on Bathsheba? Or was David just as responsible? More so? Explain.

_____

_____

_____

_____

(6) a. How did David try to trick Uriah into accepting the role of father?

_____

_____

_____

b. What happened to Bathsheba and David's first child? What was their attitude toward God in this?

_____

_____

_____

_____

(7) David realized he needed forgiveness. So, what did he do about it? What did he say in Psalm 51 about this?

_____

_____

_____

_____

_____

_____

(8) a. Who assured David of God's forgiveness?

_____

b. What exactly did this person communicate to David?

_____

_____

c. Did Bathsheba experience guilt before God? Did she repent and accept forgiveness?

_____

_____

_____

d. God blessed David and Bathsheba with a second son. What was his name and what did it mean?

_____

_____

(9) a. "A woman's inner beauty is almost always dependent upon her relationship with God." Do you agree with that statement? Why or why not?

_____

_____

_____

_____

b. Do you think Bathsheba forgave herself and became a good mother and wife? Why?

_____

_____

_____

c. What did Nathan think about Bathsheba?

_____

_____

_____

(10) a. Jesus Christ came into the world to forgive our sins. We need to accept forgiveness from him and from each other. Have you ever accepted forgiveness from Jesus? What is your part in this?

_____

_____

b. What lessons can you learn from Bathsheba?

_____

_____

_____

_____

_____

_____

_____

LESSON 5

Mary, the Mother of Jesus

NOTES

Especially helpful Scriptures about Mary are: Matthew 1:2, 12:46; Luke 1; 2; John 2:1-11; 19:25; Acts 1:14.

No woman on the face of the earth has had as much honor as Mary, the mother of Jesus. Her name has been popular in all countries. It has been given at least twenty different interpretations, the most popular being Maria, Marie, Miriam, and Marianne.

According to the Bible, Mary was a humble village woman who lived in the small town of Nazareth. It must have been an insignificant little village, for Nathanael asked, "Can there any good thing come out of Nazareth?" (John 1:46, KJV). But the greatest Man the world has ever known came out of Nazareth. We are prone to overlook where we live, where we were born, how we lived as children, but it is all very important in our training to become adults.

Mary was of the tribe of Judah and the line of David. She became the wife of Joseph, the son of Heli (Luke 3:23). Elizabeth, her cousin, honored her with the title "the mother of my Lord" and praised her as "blessed among women."

Mary, a virgin, gave birth to Christ in a miraculous way. She knew he was the Son of the living God. Later she gave birth to four sons and several daughters. The sons were James, Joseph, Judas (or Jude), and Simon (Matthew 13:55, 56; Mark 6:3). The daughters are not named in Scripture.

God did not go into a large city and pick out a socially prominent woman to bring his Son, the Savior, into the world. The gentle Mary was his choice. We get a good picture of the way Mary felt about God her Father from her song of praise in which she magnified him for regarding her lowly estate and for exalting her. Jesus was to labor and live among the common people, who were ready for him and would hear him gladly (see Luke 1:46-55).

Centuries before Mary became the mother of Jesus, it was prophesied that it would be so (Isaiah 7:14-16; 9:6, 7; Micah 5:2). Because of his early background and training by Mary, his mother, and Joseph, his carpenter stepfather, Jesus was able to love and sympathize with man as man and to be regarded by all people as the common property of all. This was a very important part of his early training and should not be overlooked.

Mary willingly yielded her body to the Lord, saying, "I am the Lord's servant, and I am willing to do whatever he wants" (Luke 1:38). We do not understand the mystery of what happened when Mary yielded up her body, but we can believe that with God nothing is impossible and accept what Scripture says about the birth of Christ. Someone has said, "Jesus Christ himself is such a miracle that it is no straining of faith to believe that his birth was also a miracle." Born of a woman, he was man, yet also divine.

There were many things Mary was not able to give her son—such as wealth or "the best education." But little is much if God is in it, and he was in Jesus his Son. Mary gave Jesus a home, and because of her character we know it was filled with love, mutual trust, and sympathetic understanding. Most of all she gave him her life. He became bone of her bone, flesh of her flesh. Her warm milk nourished him. He was her son as well as God's only Son.

Gabriel said to Mary, "The Lord is with you." This awareness of the presence of God surrounded Mary at all times. A mother who has this awareness of the presence of the living God can pass it on to her child. This is a wonderful trait; nothing is greater. I experienced this from my own dear mother and I have never forgotten it. Mary lived in the divine presence. Are you giving this to your children? Will they remember it as an outstanding characteristic of your life?

A child who is not taught to obey his parents will have trouble obeying the Lord. Mary believed this for herself and her children. She submitted to the Father's will and her son, Jesus, grew up obedient to Mary and Joseph and to his heavenly Father. Mary must have saturated her children with the record of the saints and prophets and sung God's praises daily in her home. Jesus came to know that the Scripture testified of him, that he came to earth to be the living Word.

Mary was a very special mother; God knew exactly what he was doing. He also knows just exactly what he wants you to do and what he can do for you and your family, if you will follow Mary's example. He has a plan for your life, no matter who you are, how much education you have or have not, or what your financial status is or is not. Your job is to find his will for your life, walk in obedience before him, and let him mature you and discipline your life so you can become his special treasure on earth. Will you commit your entire body, soul and spirit to him today?

The last picture we have of Mary is a gentle, heart-warming one. We find her in the upper room among the group of believers waiting for the Holy Ghost, the Comforter, to come (Acts 1:12-14). Her Son was alive, and his life had changed her. She was there as a receiver, a humble servant, along with the rest of the people, including her sons who were now believers. She is praying and believing. Wasn't it wonderful that she could have a glimpse of Jesus, her Son, glorified—that she could know the purpose of it all and that she was a contributing part of the entire plan of God to save the world.

Mary did not magnify herself—only her Lord.

QUESTIONS

(1) a. It has been suggested that no woman in the entire history of the world has been so honored and revered as Mary. Is this a

true statement in your opinion? Why or why not?

_____

_____

_____

    b.   What does Luke 1:28, 42 tell you about Mary?

_____

_____

    c.   Do you think the unbeliever as well as the believer feels she is the subject of adoration? Why or why not?

_____

_____

_____

(2) Where did Mary live as a girl? Where did she live as a married woman? Was the family considered poor, middle-class, or wealthy? Give verses to support your answer.

_____

_____

_____

(3) The story of the virgin birth appears in the Bible in two separate places. Where are these found? From whose point of view was each written?

_____

_____

_____

(4) *Challenge:* From whom do you think Luke got his point of view? (Check a commentary or Bible dictionary.) Was there more than one source?

_____
_____
_____

(5) a. In what verse does Mary find out what name she is to call her son? What does that name mean?

_____
_____

  b. Who told her? Give the verse.

_____

  c. What was Mary's answer to the one who told her, in your own words?

_____
_____
_____

  d. What does this say to you about Mary?

_____
_____

(6) What did the angel tell Mary in Luke 1:35?

_____
_____
_____

(7) How did she react to this statement from the angel?

_____

_____

_____

(8) How do the Gospels of Matthew and Luke differ in their account of the conception? Give verses.

_____

_____

_____

_____

(9) How does John 8:23 confirm Jesus' supernatural birth?

_____

_____

_____

(10) The first words of the famous *"Ave Maria"* are taken from Luke 1:28. What are they?

_____

_____

_____

(11) What does Luke 1:27 say about Mary?

_____

_____

_____

(12) a. Elizabeth, Mary's cousin, greeted her with the same salutation as that of the angel. What did she say to Mary?

_____

b. How did she address Mary in Luke 1:43?

(13) What is the passage in Luke 1:46-55 called today? Why?

(14) a. Name a psalm or two that make good companions to Luke 1:46-55.

b. What specific things does Mary talk about in this hymn of praise?

c. Do you praise God only once in a while, never, or continually? What does a spirit of praise do for you personally?

(15) What does Mark 6:3 tell you about Jesus' family? John 19:25?

(16) a. What verse assures us of Joseph's love for Mary?

b. Who were Mary's parents? Were they holy people?

(17) a. What application can you see from Luke 2:19 for yourself?

b. What did Simeon have to say about Mary in Luke 2:34?

c. Put Luke 2:34 into your own words. What does it say to you?

(18) a. What information does Luke 2:52 give you about Jesus as he grew up? What basic areas of growth do we see here?

b. What did Mary say to her son when she found him in the Temple, sitting among the doctors of law? Give the verse. What does this show about Mary?

_____

_____

_____

_____

c. What was Jesus' answer? Give the verse.

_____

_____

_____

d. What does Jesus' answer tell us about who Jesus is?

_____

_____

_____

_____

(19) a. In John 2 we find Jesus' farewell to his private life and the beginning of his public ministry. Mary was about fifty years old when she went to the feast with Jesus. For the first time he answered her not as her son, but as the Messiah. What did he call her and what did he say to her? Give the verses. Put this in your own words.

_____

_____

_____

_____

_____

b.　Do you think this was a hard test of Mary's faith? Why or why not?

_____
_____
_____

　　c.　How did Mary take this from her son? What did she tell the servant to do? From then on Mary remains in the background of Jesus' life. Why?

_____
_____
_____

(20) a.　How did Jesus show his love and concern for Mary while on the cross? Give the verses.

_____
_____
_____

　　b.　Acts 1:12-14 tells us about the Bible's last mention of Mary. Where was she? What was she doing? Why?

_____
_____
_____

　　c.　What do you think is the charm in the life of Mary? (See 2 Timothy 3:15.)

_____
_____

(21) Give several applications from Mary's life that were a blessing to you. Share the ones you have used.

LESSON 6
Review

QUESTIONS

Comment on each point below and give references for all Scriptures supporting your answer.

Lesson 1: *Tamar*.
 (1) Her selection— _____

_____

_____

 (2) Her salvation— _____

_____

_____

 (3) Her submission— _____

_____

_____

(4) Her service—

(5) Her sorrow—

(6) Her reward—

Lesson 2: *Rahab.*
(1) Her selection—

(2) Her salvation—

(3) Her submission—

(4) Her service—

(5) Her sorrow—

(6) Her reward— _____

_____

_____

Lesson 3: *Ruth.*
   (1) Her selection— _____

_____

_____

   (2) Her salvation— _____

_____

_____

   (3) Her submission— _____

_____

_____

   (4) Her service— _____

_____

_____

   (5) Her sorrow— _____

_____

_____

   (6) Her reward— _____

_____

_____

Lesson 4: *Bathsheba.*
   (1) Her selection— _____

_____

_____

(2) Her salvation— _____
_____
_____

(3) Her submission— _____
_____
_____

(4) Her service— _____
_____
_____

(5) Her sorrow— _____
_____
_____

(6) Her reward— _____
_____
_____

Lesson 5: *Mary, the mother of Jesus.*
  (1) Her selection— _____
_____
_____

  (2) Her salvation— _____
_____
_____

  (3) Her submission— _____
_____
_____

(4) Her service— _____
_____
_____

(5) Her sorrow— _____
_____
_____

(6) Her reward— _____
_____
_____

LESSON 7

The Ideal Woman

Proverbs 31:10-31

NOTES

Proverbs 31:10-31 gives a beautiful picture of female excellence and of what God wants from any woman's life, a picture of an ideal wife and mother, of her talents and her charm. This lesson will prove to be a challenge to any who take the time to read and study this passage of Scripture.

After you have read Proverbs 31, ask God to cleanse you of any sin in your life. Ask to be filled and controlled by the Holy Spirit as you study. Ask the Holy Spirit to point out to you where you have fallen short and where you need help. Be sensitive to your need, and let God lead you.

Pick out applications that are your own, and use them this week as you refer back to this lesson. God will enrich your life and abundantly bless you as you put his Word to work in your life. (Read this Scripture in the *Amplified Bible* if possible.) If you are single, these qualities can still relate to you.

QUESTIONS

(1) What are some of the characteristics of the ideal woman's spiritual life? (See Proverbs 31:10, 25, 26, 28, 29, 30.)

_____

_____

_____

_____

_____

(2) a. In verse 10, what does "virtuous" (KJV) mean? Do you qualify?

_____

_____

_____

_____

b. What do these Scriptures tell you about God's ideal woman?
12:4— _____

_____

_____

19:14— _____

_____

_____

(3) a. According to verse 11, how is the heart of the husband satisfied? Is this in everything pertaining to the husband, or is it just the spiritual part?

_____

_____

b. In verse 11, could your husband put your name in for "her" or "she"? Is God first in your life, or is your husband first? What does Luke 12:31 tell you about whom to place first in your life? Does this verse really work?

(4) What do the following Scriptures have to say about wives, or things that could be applied to wives?

1 Corinthians 11:1-10— _____

Ephesians 4:22, 24; 5:22, 24, 33— _____

Titus 2:3-5— _____

1 Peter 3:1-6— _____

(5) Read verse 12. What are evil things you can do to make the life of your husband miserable? List some of them. (Remember that sometimes the things we think are for their good are really sins and

we need to let the Holy Spirit open our eyes to them.) What do 19:13; 21:9; 27:15 add to this?

_____

_____

_____

_____

_____

(6) Write out what verses 14, 15 mean, in your own words. (Could there be a hint of monotony here?)

_____

_____

_____

_____

(7) a. As a Christian, how does God expect you to help the poor (verses 19, 20)? See also Ephesians 4:28; Hebrews 13:16.

_____

_____

_____

_____

b. What is your attitude toward the poor? Why?

_____

_____

_____

_____

(8) a. Relate verse 23 to the way we work and live today. What does 12:4 have to do with this?

_____

b. What emotions are stirred in your heart and mind when this (verse 23) happens to your husband or to any of your sons?

(9) What qualities of a homemaker are found in verses 13-27?

(10) a. What do verses 15, 17 tell you about your own interests and talents? See also Luke 12:42; Romans 12:11.

b. Can you find four verses in this passage that speak of creativity? What do they say?

c. Find four verses about being businesslike. What do they say?

_____
_____
_____

(11) God wants *you* to have a ministry to others. What three verses here say this?

_____
_____
_____

(12) Can you name a woman in the Bible who best exemplifies some of the ideal woman's characteristics? Give reasons why you think of her this way.

_____
_____
_____
_____
_____

(13) List several characteristics or qualities that you found in God's ideal woman that you feel are missing in your own life, and that you would like God to help you acquire to make you a well-balanced, whole Christian person.

_____
_____
_____
_____

(14) Will you share this list with your husband or with a close Christian friend if you are single? Will the two of you ask God to begin his work of grace in you?

_____

(15) What characteristics are given in this lesson that you feel you have? List them from Scripture and thank God for each one of them. Pray that he will continue to perfect the work he has begun in you (Philippians 1:6).

_____

_____

_____

_____

(16) Has verse 28 ever happened to you? Has your husband blessed you? Have your children blessed you? What does this do for you? How does it make you feel? (If you are not married, what does it do to and for you when a friend, a neighbor, or an enemy does this to you?) Do you bless others as well?

_____

_____

_____

_____

(17) Would you like to have God say to you, as you meet him in Heaven, what is said to the daughters in verse 29? What did God say?

_____

_____

_____

(18) a. Is God going to praise you for your beauty and for all the favors you have given here on earth? What will he praise you for? Give the verses.

_____

_____

_____

_____

b. According to verse 31, what is God going to give you? How are you going to "stack up" with this verse? Do you have both of the things mentioned?

___

(19) Give one outstanding thought you received for yourself from this passage in Proverbs.

___